WORSHIP
BRINGS RAIN

Temitope Odetunde

WORSHIP BRINGS RAIN

Copyright © 2019 by Temitope Odetunde

Publishing Name
Rio-Influencia Publishing

First Edition
ISBN-13: 978-1-9162072-0-2 - E-book
ISBN-13: 978-1-9162072-1-9 – Paperback

Printed in the United Kingdom and the United States of America

Unless otherwise stated, all scripture quotes are taken from the King James Version; with emphasis added or paraphrased.

Publishing Consultants
Vike Springs Publishing Ltd.
www.vikesprings.com

For further information or contact Temi please send an email to: a4asoto@gmail.com. Temi's books are available at special discounts when purchased in bulk for promotions or as donations for educational, inspirational and training purposes

Limit Of Liability/ Disclaimer Of Warranty

Acknowledgement

I am immensely grateful to all the lecturers at Kings College of Excellence, who have inspired and contributed to my development during my Diploma in Christian Ministry, thank you.

In writing this book, I was privileged to have like-minded people who contributed their knowledge and added their input to this book.

I was fortunate to have the support of Mrs Sophia Hunte-St Rose, who inspired me to write and to allow myself to envision my potential in producing a book. I want to thank Dr Derin Adegboga of Top Achievers' Programme, who helped with proofreading and editing the manuscript.

I want to say thank you, Minister Soji Otudeko, for writing the foreword within this book; I am grateful for your time.

Finally, thank you to the set man and the angels of the KICC family, Pastor Matthew and Pastor Yemisi, for preaching and challenging us to be all that we can be in God.

Foreword

This book is about the spirit, the heart and the art of worship.

Temitope writes like someone who has experienced worship in the deepest place of the holy of holies and wants to encourage the reader to a deeper level of worship, right into God's presence continually.

Jesus said, "the time comes, and now is that those that worship God must worship Him in truth and in spirit". This book will help you understand what true worship is and how to worship God in the spirit.

I commend this book to you; it will help your worship life.

Soji Otudeko
Pastor, Vine Church London
Lecturer, Kings College of Excellence

Table of Contents

Made for Greatness

Before you were formed in your mother's womb,
I knew you
Before the oceans were created, I gave birth to
you
Before I created anything else, I created you
You are special to me; you were made for great-
ness
On the day you were born
No one had the slightest interest in you
You were helpless, and no one to care for you
I came by and saw you; I said live
This is because you were made for greatness

You were naked, but I covered you
I wrapped my cloak of love around you
I made a covenant with you
You became royalty
You became exclusively mine
This is because you were made for greatness

I have made you wonderfully complex
Intricately stitched together
You are indeed a masterpiece
In me, you are thoroughly furnished
Because my seed of greatness is in you

So, as you stand before me today
With worry, doubt and fear in your heart
Wondering what tomorrow holds for you
The question remains unanswered
whose report will you believe

You see my covenant I will not break

I will not alter that which I said about you
For I am the Lord who called you
I will establish, strengthen and settle you
I will make you what you ought to be
Eternal excellence a joy of many generations
Because you were made for greatness.

The story

The year (2019) is unusual. I was tired of activity without results and promises without manifestation. I analysed and reviewed all areas of my life, and I noticed certain patterns which did not line up with the word of God. I concluded that if this faith works, then it must work for me.

I was privileged to attend the Kings College of Excellence, and the module right at the beginning of the year was the ministry of the Holy Spirit. I was looking forward to this module, and there I was on a dark cold Thursday evening in my usual seat waiting to catch the revelation for that evening. The lecture was intense, challenging and thought-provoking. The tutor gave us two assignments, which are: 1) Pray an extra 15 minutes a day in this manner – say, "Holy Spirit, I want to know you more; please empower me". 2) To read the book of Acts five times.

As I left the classroom that evening, I decided that I will not miss any of the sessions, and I committed to complete the homework as instructed. The Holy Spirit honoured my commitment, and for each lecture, I had a testimony about the ministry of the Holy Spirit in my personal life. The move of the Holy Spirit was strong and overwhelming in all the sessions.

As the module concluded, I made up my mind that this will be a daily experience, compared to the irregular pattern I have had in the past. In one of my prayer times, shortly after this module, I asked God a question: "When will Your word be fulfilled in my life?" To my amazement, God challenged me with a question of His own: "What do you know about worship?" I remembered that in Job 38, God posed a series of questions to Job. I know He was not looking for an answer, but He was calling me higher.

One of the modules we studied at Kings College of Excellence equipped us with methods and tools to study the scriptures. I decided that I can only answer God's question from His word, so I did a topical study of the word 'worship' using as many Bible study tools I could find. I was intrigued as to why God seemed so perturbed with the children of Israel each time they disobeyed and pursued other gods. I was fascinated that God withheld rain when the children of Israel decided to worship other gods. God started to reveal the scripture to me in an unusual way.

This book is about God teaching me about worship and what it means to worship Him as a true worshipper. It originated from my arduous pursuit to establish the direction in which God was guiding me in this time and season. I pray as you read my journey of discovery to unravel the answer, you will gain valuable insight on how to worship the Creator of our universe.

⟫ 1 ⟪

YOU SHALL HAVE NO OTHER GOD

Worship is defined as an act of reference for someone of high-ranking or a deity; it also means to bow down. The Greek word for worship is proskuneo, meaning to "kiss", or the Hebrew word sometimes used for worship is shachah, which means to fall down, depress or prostrate. Merriam-webster.com defines bow down as showing weakness by agreeing to demand or following the orders of someone or something. Cambridge English dictionary.com also defines bow down to show respect to someone and acknowledge that they are more powerful than you. Biblical scriptures also embrace the words bow down, and they are found several times within the Bible, which encouraged me to examine their meaning in greater detail.

I took time to explore the definition of worship because, during my study using the strong concordance, I came across these words "BOW DOWN" numerous times, especially when God was giving the children of Israel the mandate for living after they came out of the land of Egypt. I was intrigued as to why God seemed so perturbed with the children of Israel each time they disobeyed and pursued other gods. In my meditation time, I remember questioning God about His obsession with the children of Israel, about them bowing down to another god. At that junction, the Holy Spirit clearly intimated the following,

> *"Anytime you bow to anything other than God, you inadvertently try to make the God in you to bow to the work of His hands. God cannot be made to bow to other gods".*

The Holy Spirit expounded this revelation to me through God's word in Genesis 2:7: "God formed man from the dust of the earth, and He breathed into man and man became a living soul." Job further attested to this truth in Job 33:4 and said, "the spirit of God has made me, and the breath of God gives me life".

When man fell in the Garden of Eden, the spirit of God in man died (separation from God), but when a man receives Christ (the gift of salvation), the spirit of God in him comes alive. Therefore, if a man bows to other gods after receiving the gift of salvation, he is inadvertently making the Christ in him bow, and this is construed as idolatry. He is declaring that God is weak, and this other "thing" is more powerful than the Christ in him. In Exodus 34:14,God specifically told the children of Israel not to worship another god, and He also told them the consequences of disobeying Him in Deuteronomy 8:19 they will be destroyed.

Obedience is achieved when there is submission to authority (another word for authority is supremacy or sovereignty). When a person accepts or concedes to a superior force or will of another person, this is interpreted as submission. **According to the definition above, the sin of Adam in the Garden of Eden is that he accepted or conceded to the will of whom he considered as having a superior force. In other words, he bowed down to the devil** therefore God drove him and his wife out of the Garden of Eden. The devil was created to worship God, but he was thrown out of heaven because he took that which belonged to God and ascribed it to himself.

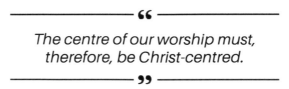

The centre of our worship must, therefore, be Christ-centred.

We expose ourselves to the following anytime we step out of this command:

Separation from God, which exposes a man to shame.(Psalm97:7)

We provoke the anger of God. (Jeremiah 25:6)

We are not useful to our God. (Jeremiah 13:10)

Further scriptures to consider:

Deuteronomy 11:16

Deuteronomy 30:17

1 Kings 9:6

1 Kings 12:30

2 Chronicles 7:19

Psalm 81:9

2

RITUALISTIC WORSHIP

As I studied this subject of worship, I came across the scripture where God told the children of Israel to draw near, but they refused. They preferred to worship from a distance. Even though Moses encouraged them to draw near, they maintained their position (Exodus 20:21). God saw the condition of their heart; therefore, in Exodus 24:1, God said, "And Moses alone shall come near the Lord, but they (the children of Israel) shall not come near; nor shall the people go up with him."I studied the word distance, and I found that there were several meanings; however, I will focus primarily on the one below:

To be emotionally separated

Jesus said in Matthew 15:8: "These people honour me with their lips, but their heart is far from me." Isaiah 29:13 (Good News Translation) states, **"These people claim to worship me, but their words are meaningless, and their hearts are somewhere else. Their religion is nothing but human rules and traditions, which they have simply memorized"**.

Some worship services are sadly characterised by a set of fast and slow songs that we are all so acquainted with. We have memorised the programme of worship and can recite it with our eyes closed. We know the song people want to hear and the ones that will bring the right emotion in the room, irrespective of whether God is present or not. I am always amazed to see people on their phones, taking a selfie, greeting their friends, doing everything else except worshipping during the allocated time set for congregational worship. We are very creative when singing different artist's songs, learning the cords, styles, dynamics and lyrics that we are unfortunately stifling the birth of new songs during our worship. Occasionally, we get the new song, but it's time for the next thing on the agenda, or we change the song because we must sing that favourite song on our worship set. John 4:23 says, "But the hour comes, and now is when the true worshippers shall worship the Father in spirit and in truth: for the Father seeks such to worship him."

Our worship should flow from the guidance of the Holy Spirit.

For our worship to be acceptable before God, we must critically check the following:

1. The worshipper must be **born of the Spirit**. John 3:5 says, "Jesus answered, 'verily, verily, I say unto thee, unless a man is born of water and the spirit, he cannot enter into the kingdom of heaven.'"This suggests to me that for our worship to be accepted before the throne of heaven and to worship in the spirit as specified in John 4:23, we must be born of the spirit.

―――――――――― **"** ――――――――――

We can safely say an unbeliever cannot worship God because they are not born of the spirit of God.

―――――――――― **"** ――――――――――

2. The worshipper must be **led by the Spirit**. John 4:24 (Contemporary English Translation) says, "God is spirit, and those who worship God must be led by the spirit to worship Him according to the truth". Good News Translation says, "God is Spirit, and only by the power of His Spirit can people worship Him as He really is".

―――――――――― **"** ――――――――――

To worship in the Spirit, you must be led by the Spirit.

―――――――――― **"** ――――――――――

1 Corinthians 2:11says, "You are the only One who knows what is in your mind, and God's Spirit is the only One who knows what is in God's mind."We will only know the song God wants to hear and the ones His people need when the Spirit leads us. After all, we are singing to Him, and our worship is for Him.

3. The worshipper must **worship by the power of the Holy Spirit**. Philippians 3:3 (Contemporary English Version) says, "But

we are the ones who are truly circumcised because we worship by the power of God's spirit..." We are not to worship through the flesh or by the power of the flesh but by the power of the Spirit.

"

We are not to worship through the flesh or by the power of the flesh but by the power of the Spirit.

"

According to the scriptures, we must be **born** of the Spirit, **led** by the Spirit and **worship by the power of the Spirit**. Whatever we are doing outside of these truths is not worship but mere ritual, entertainment or performance. In the presence of true worship, the word of God is released, which reveals hidden secrets, and convicts people of their sin (1 Corinthian 14:25). God is seeking true worshippers who are circumcised and are born of Him, who are led by the spirit and who will worship by the power of the Spirit of God.

In Acts 13:22, "After removing Saul, He made David their king. He testified concerning him: 'I have found David son of Jesse a man after My own heart; he will do everything I want him to do.'" We saw from the scriptures that David is a worshipper. He worshipped God with everything he had; he danced before God foolishly and gave God perpetual praise. David praised God seven times a day (Psalm 119:164), and his life of worship helps him to write such a thought-provoking psalm, which we read today. A quote from an unknown source reads: "We human beings may be looking for new and improved ways to worship, but God is not. He does not want experts in worship; what God wants is people who will follow His instructions every time they approach Him."

3

THE PRIEST

IN the old and new testament, we saw how God called His own people into the office of a priest. Exodus 19:6 says, "Unto me you shall be a kingdom of priests and a holy nation. Revelation 5: 8-14 attests to this and says, "We (the redeemed) are a kingdom of priests to our God."The scriptures make us understand that the primary role of a priest is to minister to the Lord (Exodus 28:1). The purpose of the garment of the priest is to consecrate him so that he can minister to the Lord (Exodus 28:3-4). The purpose of the anointing, the consecration and the sanctification of a priest is so that he can minister to the Lord (Exodus 28:41). The word minister means to tend, to care for, to serve, to wait on and to attend to the need of someone.

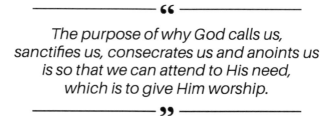

The purpose of why God calls us, sanctifies us, consecrates us and anoints us is so that we can attend to His need, which is to give Him worship.

This book will not be able to cover what it means to be a priest fully, but there are specific guidelines as to the role of a priest, how they should dress and behave in Exodus chapter 25.

The first requirement of a priest in the old testament is that they have a holy garment. A garment is a form of **identity;** for example, a bridal garment helps us to identify the bride. There is a **purpose** for every garment; for example, there is a garment used for celebration, there is a garment of judgement used by prisoners, and there is a garment to recognise certain positions. A garment is a **sign of authority**; for example, a metropolitan police officer in the United Kingdom fully clothed in his uniform(garment) giving direction and standing at a major junction cannot be overlooked because he or she is operating under the authority of the metropolitan police of United Kingdom. Disobedience to that authority will carry certain consequences. The first time the word garment was mentioned in the Bible was when God made a garment for Adam and Eve after they sinned against God. The garments covered their shame and vulnerability.

Exodus 28:2 says, "And you shall make holy garments for Aaron your brother for honour and dignity." (Some Bible versions say for glory and beauty). The word dignity also means a state of being worthy or a state of quality. The word honour can also mean distinction, glory, integrity, uprightness, righteousness, goodness, faithfulness. A priest's garment is such that when people see it, they will see glory, beauty, integrity, uprightness, righteousness, goodness, faithfulness. These attributes resemble the fruits of the Holy Spirit and will only manifest in us when we put on Christ.

As a 21ˢᵗ century believer, people will only see these attributes in us when we start to work in the Spirit and allow Him to lead us.

Exodus 28:41 says, "...you shall **anoint** them (Aaron and his sons), **consecrate** them and **sanctify** them that they may minister to Me as priest." To consecrate means to declare a thing or a person holy and dedicated to God. To sanctify means to be approved, to declare hallow, to be justified, to be cleansed, to be redeemed, to be absolved(to be declared free from guilt, obligation or punishment).

The day an unbeliever accepts Jesus Christ into their life as Lord and Saviour, they are justified and cleansed from sin.

However, to stay justified and to continue in a life of holiness, one must work in the Spirit. The eye of the Lord cannot behold iniquity, and we cannot achieve holiness in our own strength because our righteousness is like a filthy rag before God.

In Leviticus, God spoke through Moses to the descendants of Aaron, who were of the priest lineage that whoever that hath any blemish must not approach the altar of God to offer a sacrifice. In this passage, God was talking more about a physical defect, but if we are the offering/sacrifice, God wants us to be holy without sin, no spot or wrinkles so that our worship will be acceptable before Him. In Exodus 30:18-21, Aaron and his son (the priest lineage) are instructed by God that they must wash their feet and hands in water before entering the tabernacle of God or before approaching the altar of God.

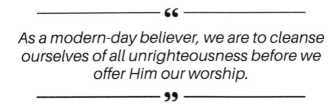

As a modern-day believer, we are to cleanse ourselves of all unrighteousness before we offer Him our worship.

Matthew 5:23-24 says, "Therefore if you bring your gift to the altar, and there remember that your brother has something against you, leave your gift there before the altar, and go your way. First, be reconciled to your brother, and then come and offer your gift." We cannot approach the throne of God with unclean hands; our worship will be defiled, and it will be an abomination to God.

Worship is led by the priest as seen in Exodus 30:7-8, "Aaron must burn fragrant incense on the altar every morning when he tends the lamp, he must burn incense again when he lights the lamp at twilight so incense will regularly burn before the Lord for the generation to come." Offering animals as a burnt offering and other ceremonial sacrifices was a major part of worship for the Israelites. God specified that there must be daily offerings, which is a form of worship for the children of Israel, and this must be done twice a day (morning for a sweet aroma to God and at twilight).God wants His people to open the day and close the day in worship (Exodus 29:39, 42). God promised that when they bring their offering, He will meet with them and speak to them. Under the new covenant ratified by the blood of Jesus Christ, we are delivered from the ritualistic laws.

——————————— 66 ———————————

When a believer accepts Christ as their personal Lord and Saviour, they are the sacrifice; their entire being is for God's worship.

——————————— 99 ———————————

In Romans, the Bible says, "And so, dear brothers and sisters, I plead with you to give your bodies to God because of all he has done for you. Let them be a living and holy sacrifice – the kind he will find acceptable. This is truly the way to worship him" (Roman 12:1 New Living Translation). Just as God wants the children of Israel in the old testament to open the day and close the day in worship, our day must start in worship to our Father, thanking Him for a brand-new day, and we close the day thanking Him for the opportunities of the day. God promised that when we worship Him daily, He will meet with us, and He will speak to us.

God also commanded that this offering of worship must be made according to God's precept - the animal offered must be of high quality.

> *If we are now the sacrifice for worship, our life must be pure and acceptable before Him.*

This means worship is much more than what happens on Sunday for 30 minutes; it's a daily walk with God. In Malachi, God commanded the priest and warned them about how to behave and live their life as a priest of the most high God - A priest must revere God and stand in awe of His name. A priest is called to walk with God, living a good and righteous life, be upright and should turn many away from lives of sin (Malachi 2:6). The lips of a priest ought to preserve God's knowledge because he is the representative of God (Malachi 2:7). As priests, we are to offer worship to our God, who is the only One worthy to receive our worship. Unbelievers will be converted to Christ by observing our life of worship.

In the book of Leviticus, we saw that the sacrifice of the people of God placed on the altar was consumed by the fire that comes from the glory of God in the tabernacle, and this is an indication that their offering was accepted. The priest is also preserved. "And he shall take a censer full of burning coal of fire **from off the altar before the Lord.**" Verse 13 says, "And he shall put the incense upon the fire before the Lord, that the cloud of the incense may cover the mercy seat that is upon the testimony, that he (the priest) die not" (Leviticus 16:12 - 13). As long as the priest abides by this directive, he is preserved. We were introduced to some people in the scriptures who did not follow the prescribed pattern, and they suffered the consequences. Nadab and Abihu, Aaron's oldest sons, took their own censer (not the one from the altar before the Lord), put fire in it (not the fire from off the altar before the Lord) and put incense thereon (they did not put the incense upon the fire before the Lord).Therefore, God rejected their sacrifice because they did not obey the instructions God gave them. It was an unholy fire; therefore, fire came out from the presence of the Lord and consumed them, and they died before the Lord. Moses later explained to Aaron why God had done such a harsh thing. Then Moses said to Aaron, "This is what the Lord was speaking about when He said, 'All who serve me must respect My holiness; I will reveal My glory to My people"' (Leviticus 10:3, Good News Translation). Theologians said that the offering of Aaron's sons was the first time sacrifices were being offered on the altar. Therefore, God was not going to let the other priests who will serve after them think that it is acceptable to disregard the precept given by God.

—————————— 66 ——————————

*God is not going to change His protocol
to suit us; we must align ourselves with
His directive.*

—————————— 99 ——————————

The Bible also told us about a king who started
with God, and God marvellously helped him. King
Uzziah's fame spread far and wide; then pride
entered his heart. The Bible says he entered the
temple of the Lord to burn incense on the altar
of incense. Azariah, the priest, confronted him
and told him it is not his place to burn incense to
the Lord. This role is for the priest, who has been
consecrated to burn incense. They even told him
that his offering would not be accepted. King
Uzziah did not listen; instead, He got angry with
the priest. The Bible says while he was raging at
the priest, right there, leprosy broke out on his
forehead, and he had leprosy until the day he
died (2 Chronicles 26: 10-21).

Have you ever wondered why there are many
sick and asleep in our churches today? There
is not much difference between the people of
the world and the children of the kingdom?
Can it be that we are not following the protocol
of heaven, and we are offering God strange fire
on His altar? Therefore, people come to church
with their sickness and disease, and they leave
the same way. I have wondered and asked God

why is there no power in our churches as we have heard of in the days of old. Can it be that we are now full of ourselves? Are there some that are not priests but are pretending to be priests? We are not sanctified and consecrated to Him, but we are asking for His fire. We are no longer discerning the body of Christ; therefore, we are bringing judgement on ourselves. I Corinthians 11:30 says, "That is why many among you are weak and sick, and a number of you have fallen asleep." Another version said a considerable number of you are dying.

66

Everyone ought to examine themselves before they come to worship as it is a dangerous thing to offer carnal worship originating from the brokenness of your spirit.

99

Our fire must come from His altar, not the one we obtained from other foreign sources. Our prayer must be, do it again in our times, Lord, the great deeds You used to do (Habakkuk3:2).

The golden lamp stand in God's tabernacle in the old testament was placed on the southside in the holy place. It is said that the lampstand was the only source of light in the tabernacle. One of the duties of the priest in the old testament is to keep the lamp of the tabernacle burning before the Lord daily (Exodus 27:21). God also commanded that the children of Israel must bring pure oil of pressed olive for the light, to cause the lamp to burn continually (Exodus 27:20). Aaron and his sons must tend the lamp. "And the fire on the altar shall be kept burning on it; it shall not be put out. And the priest shall burn wood on it every morning and lay the burnt offering in order on it; and he shall burn on it the fat of the peace offering." "A perpetual fire shall burn on the altar; it shall never go out" (Leviticus 6:12-13). John, in Revelation 1:20, tells us that the lampstand is the local church; as priests, we are to keep the light of the local church burning. I dear say that the reason why the light of Christ is out in some of our churches is because the priests are distracted and are busy building their own empire and they are no longer tending the lamp. As commanded by God, believers are meant to bring pure oil (through the power of the Holy Spirit) to ensure the lamp of the local church burns continually. Jesus Christ said we are the light of the world, and we are to display our light so that it can give light to everyone.

— 66 —

We are representatives of God and the body of Christ; therefore, our light must shine continually so that unbelievers may see our good deeds and glorify God.

— 99 —

The magnificent God

My God is too much
He does miraculous things
My life tells stories of His mighty acts
He is The Magnificent God

The name of my God is amazing
That's because He is the ancient of days
Generations stand in awe of Him
He is The Magnificent God

The Lord is gracious to me
There are no boundaries to His greatness
I regularly enjoy His goodness
He is The Magnificent God

There is none like my God
Notable miracle He has done
His beauty and splendour is second to none
He is The Magnificent God

Let me describe this God to you
He is immortal and the invisible God
He is faithful and the famous one
He is extraordinary and the exalted
He is The Magnificent God

Why don't you invite this exceptional God
into your life
The only One who can secure your eternity
He will give you an extreme makeover
Together we can magnify The Magnificent God.

4

HEAVENLY WORSHIP

As part of my quest to understand what worship is about, I felt strongly to investigate what the Bible says about heavenly worship. In both the old and new testament, we see many references to worship in heaven.

The book of Revelation, chapters 4 and 5, gives us a little insight into heavenly worship. The book tells us about God's throne, and John described the One who sat on the throne and those around the throne.

Revelation 4:8 - The four living creatures, each having six wings, were full of eyes around and within. And they do not rest day or night, saying:

"Holy, holy, holy, Lord God Almighty, Who was and is and is to come!"

In this verse, we see that there is continuous worship in heaven - unceasing worship of God. This means there is no end to this worship: the worship is constant, the worship is uninterrupted, the worship is not occasional, it is not half-hearted, and there is no reduction in the intensity of their worship. Our worship must resemble the worship in heaven - Matthew 6:10 says, "Let Your kingdom come, Your will be done on earth as it is in heaven".

Isaiah also gave us a picture of the worship in heaven in Isaiah 6:1-4, which reads: "In the year King Uzziah died, I saw the Lord sitting on a throne, high and lifted up, and the train of His robe filled the temple. Above it stood seraphim;

each one had six wings: with two, he covered his feet, and with two, he flew. And one cried to another and said: 'Holy, holy, holy is the Lord of hosts; The whole earth is full of His glory!'"

Just like John, Isaiah saw the Lord sitting on a throne, high and lifted up, and the train of His robe filled the temple. In the old testament times when kings went to battle and won, they cut off a piece of the defeated king's robe and joined it to the robe of the victorious king. The length of a king's robe in the old testament is an indication of how many victories he had won and the kingdom he had subdued. I want you to imagine the length of the robe of our God, the One who conquered sin and death and defeated the enemy of our soul and purchased us with His blood. The creatures, the elders and the angels in heaven cannot but bow down and worship in awe of Him because of His glory and splendour. In Isaiah and the book of Revelation, we are told that the creatures covered their faces and feet – just like Moses was not able to behold the glory of God, and the creatures were not able to behold the glory emanating from the One who sits on the throne. In both Isaiah and Revelation, they cried, "Holy, holy, holy is the Lord." The English root word for holy is whole. Whole means the totality of a thing, uncondensed, full, unreduced, intact, a thing that is complete in itself, every part, the sum, total, the distinctness of something. When the creatures cry 'holy' during their worship, they are saying the One who sits on the throne is complete in Himself; He is the totality of everything, and He is distinct, lacking nothing. They were speaking of who God is and His character: You are holy, You are worthy, You are mighty - who was, who is and is to come. They give glory and honour and thanks to the One who sits on the throne.

Revelation 4:10 - the twenty-four elders fall down before Him who sits on the throne and worship Him who lives forever and ever and cast their crowns before the throne.

During the worship service in heaven, we saw that the 24 elders fell on their face and worshipped the One who sits on the throne. There is a sense of rejoicing and gladness as you read about the worship that goes on in heaven. In Nehemiah 9:6, the Bible says, "The heavenly host bows down before you, Lord." David says in the book of Psalms 19:1, "The heavens declare the glory of God, and the firmament shows His handiwork." The elders falling down suggest a sense of humility, not only that they cast their crown (their achievement and trophies) before the throne and worship God, but that they stood in awe and gave highest esteem and respect to the One who sat on the throne. If the elders in heaven are bowing down to worship God, then we the sons of men must show greater honour and respect as we come to offer our worship to our maker and Lord.

Revelation 5:8 -9: Now when He had taken the scroll, the four living creatures and the twenty-four elders fell down before the Lamb, each having a harp. And they sang a new song, saying: "You are worthy to take the scroll and to open its seals. For You were slain and have redeemed us to God by Your blood, out of every tribe and tongue and people and nation".

In the worship service in heaven, there is a harp, which is a string instrument. There is good music in heaven, and I believe the worship is not sluggish but a lively worship experience. In the worship service of heaven, they sing new songs about how Jesus redeemed us to God through his blood. The twenty-four elders were raving about God's ability (You are worthy), they spoke of his achievement (You have redeemed us to God by Your blood), they spoke about the extent of His exploit (You have redeemed us to God by Your blood out of every tribe and tongue and people and nation).

Revelation 5:11 says, "The whole of heaven worshipped and praised God with one voice" (note that the voice is in the singular; they worshipped in one accord).

It is clear from the scriptures that the hosts of heaven are excited, rejoicing and in awe of God and worshipped Him. Revelation 5:11-12 (NIV) says, "Then I looked and heard the voice of many angels, and ten thousands upon thousands, and ten thousand times ten thousand (one million). They encircled the throne and the living creatures and the elders in a **loud voice** they were saying: 'worthy is the lamb who was slain...'" Can you imagine over a million people in a room shouting all at the same time? How noisy would that be? They are not mumbling during their worship, they are not sloppy, neither are they distracted during their worship.

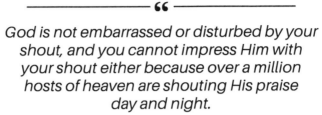

God is not embarrassed or disturbed by your shout, and you cannot impress Him with your shout either because over a million hosts of heaven are shouting His praise day and night.

The book of Revelation tells us that in heaven, they worship God with harp, holding golden bowls full of incense (Revelation 5:10). The Bible makes us understand that the incense in the golden bowl is the prayer of the saints. This means our supplication in the place of prayer must be accompanied by worship, not grumbling because our worship will bring our prayer before the throne of God.

Revelation 5:13 - And every creature which is in heaven and on the earth and under the earth and such as are in the sea, and all that are in them, I heard saying:

*"Blessing and honour and glory and power
Be to Him who sits on the throne,
And to the Lamb, forever and ever!"*

The worship in heaven consists of every creature in heaven, on earth, under the earth and in the sea boasting about the God of the whole universe. This means when we worship, we join the host of heaven in worship. Our worship is not in isolation; we are joining heaven in magnifying the One who sits on the throne. We can join the worship service of heaven because Revelation 5:10 says, "He has caused us to become a kingdom of priests to our God, the one who is authorised to offer up a sacrifice of praise and worship because of the shed blood of Christ."

5

Before You Worship

Worship is a powerful weapon in the hands of any believer and congregation. Our private and corporate worship should mirror that of heaven, as seen in Revelation 4 and 5. In the pattern of worship in heaven, there are certain features observed, which we must bear in mind as we come to offer our worship, these are:

The Throne

A time of worship is a time we approach His throne of grace. There must be a recognition of a heavenly throne and the One who is sitting on it. As we worship, we must come with an understanding that we are coming before the throne of the King of kings and the Lord of lords, the triumphant One – The Most High, Creator of heaven and earth. We must humble ourselves as we worship before His throne, laying aside our trophies, achievement and accolades. The heavenly creatures cover their faces and feet to show humility, and our posture in worship should be like this – as it is in heaven, let it be on earth.

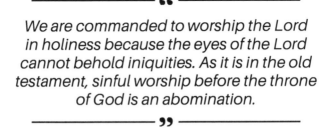

We are commanded to worship the Lord in holiness because the eyes of the Lord cannot behold iniquities. As it is in the old testament, sinful worship before the throne of God is an abomination.

Psalm 5:7 admonishes us to worship in love, reverence and fear. Psalm 99:5 and 7 tell us to go to God's dwelling place and worship at His holy mountain. 1 Chronicles 16:29 and Psalm 29:2 say, "Ascribe greatness to the Lord, give Him glory and worship His holiness and majesty." I have not visited a king's palace before, but I was told when you come before a king who is on his throne, you must approach the throne with reverence and pay homage.

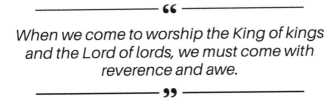

When we come to worship the King of kings and the Lord of lords, we must come with reverence and awe.

He is the God of the universe, the One who rules the heavens and the earth. The protocol of heaven is that when we become cleansed by the blood, we must then understand who He is and who we are – we are priests (Revelation 5:10).

Join the heavenly host in worship

The worship in heaven consists of every creature in heaven, on earth, under the earth and in the sea, as seen in Revelation 5:13. Psalm 69:34 says, "Let heaven and earth praise Him, The seas and everything that moves in them." This was affirmed again in Psalm 148:4, which says, "Praise Him, you heavens of heavens and you waters above the heavens." This means when we worship, we join the host of heaven in worship. I believe, therefore, God made sure the whole earth doesn't sleep and wake at the same time so that heaven and earth can be in continuous worship service.

———————— " ————————

There is always someone praising God every second. This is a powerful moment, and anything can happen when we come knowing that we are joining the host of heaven to worship God.

———————— " ————————

Boast of the King - Hallal

We saw as part of the heavenly worship; they boast of God – Holy, holy is the Lord God Almighty. Our worship should be about raving about the King of the universe, who set us apart and saved us so that we can worship Him. Psalm 34:1-3 (KJV): "I will bless the Lord at all times: His praise shall continually be in my mouth. My soul shall make her boast in the Lord: the humble shall hear thereof and be glad. O magnify the Lord with me and let us exalt His name together." Psalm 20:7 says, "Some boast in chariots and some in horses, but we will boast in the name of the Lord our God." David gave God vehement worship as he brings the ark of the covenant back to its resting place in Israel (1 Chronicles 16:4). This is a time to recall the goodness of the Lord and all He has done.

Bow and kneel before the king – Shabach / Barak

We saw as part of the heavenly worship, they bowed and worshipped the One who sits on the throne - the 24 elders and the heavenly creatures fell on their faces and worshipped the One who sits on the throne. David says we should bow down and worship and kneel before the Lord, our Maker. (Psalm 95:6). Bowing down must first happen in our hearts before there is a physical manifestation.

Worship the king with instruments – Zamar

As part of the heavenly worship, we saw the creatures and the 24 elders worship using a harp – a stringed instrument. Psalm 150:3-5 says, "Praise Him with the sounding of the trumpet, praise Him with the harp and lyre, praise Him with timbral and dancing, praise Him with the strings and pipe, praise Him with the clash of cymbals, praise Him with resounding cymbals."

---------------- 66 ----------------

Heavenly worship is lively, so get used to it on earth, or you might have a suck when you get to heaven.

---------------- 99 ----------------

In the old testament, the children of Israel brought back the ark of the covenant of the Lord with sounds of horns, trumpets, cymbals, harps and lyres raving about the God of heaven, who gave them victory over their enemies (2 Chronicles 15:28).

Shout about the King – Ruwa / Ranan

The Host of heaven is shouting with a loud voice the praise of the king. Revelation 5:12: Saying with a loud voice: "Worthy is the Lamb who was slain to receive power and riches and wisdom, and strength and honour and glory and blessing!" David said, "Shout joyfully to the Lord, all the earth: break forth and sing for joy and sing praises." David says in Psalm 47:1, "Shout to the Lord with the voice of triumph." We must shout of His saving power, shout of the victory He gave us, shout about who He is - don't be quiet: SHOUT.

Sing about the King - Tehillah

Psalm 66:4 says, "The whole earth should worship and sing praises to the name of the Lord." Our worship should involve spontaneous praise, new songs, songs that talk about the glory of our God, songs about God's majesty, sovereignty, His dominion, His wisdom and mighty works and our trust in Him. Sing about His strength, His righteousness, kindness, His unfailing love, His promises and salvation. The Bible says it is good to give thanks unto the Lord Most High.

Lift your hand and clap to the king— Macha / Yadah / Todah

The word of God encourages us to lift our hand and clap in worship of our King and Lord. The psalmist says to lift up your hands in the sanctuary and bless the Lord – and our hands be lifted up as the evening sacrifice. We saw in Nehemiah that the children of Israel lifted up their hands, and they bowed their heads and worshipped the Lord with their faces to the ground (Nehemiah 8:6). We saw Solomon stood before the altar of God and spread forth his hands towards heaven in worship (1 Kings 8:22). Worship the Lord with your hand raised – it is also a way to say to God, "I surrender to Your will and plan for me".

Dance before the King – Alats / Karar

David, the man after God's heart, encourage us to praise His name with a dance. In 2 Samuel 6:14-15, we see that David danced with all his might to thank God for returning the Ark of the covenant to its resting place. Psalm 149:3-4 says, "Let them praise His name with dancing and make music to Him with timbral and harp. "

Declaring the King's promises–Qara/ Qal / Chayah

John worshipped because of the revelation of things he was shown, although they have not manifested. Abraham worshipped after he had been visited and given a message that he will bear a son. Our worship should also involve speaking about His promises, even though we cannot see it yet, but our worship proves to God that we believe His word and trust Him that He will not fail.

6

THE RAIN

Tʜᴇ word of God through Zechariah declared that if the children of Israel did not worship the king (God), they would have no rain. Deuteronomy 11:14, "Then I will give you the rain for your land in its season, the early rain and the latter rain, that you may gather in your grain, your new wine and your oil."Verse 13, however, tells us that we will only get these promises when we obey, which we defined earlier as submission to authority, supremacy or sovereignty, or accepting or conceding to a superior force or will of another person. I pondered over this scripture and considered carefully what this might mean in the life of a believer. This led me to research about the rain to gain some knowledge and deep understanding of rain.

Rain is condensed moisture of the atmosphere falling in separate drops. Wikipedia documented that most of the freshwater on earth comes by rain. Some countries experience rain regularly. An example is Iceland; hence, the land is such a green country. It is said that the wettest place in the world is Mawsynram, and the second wettest place in the world is also in India (Cherrapunji). There are a few characteristics of rain I would like to explore in this book. They are:

The amount (quantity) of rain – The amount of rain experienced in a place can be little or small, depending on how much moisture is evaporated from the earth. The amount of rain experienced will dictate the wetness of the soil. The amount of worship (moisture) offered up to God depends on the amount of rain experienced by a worshipper. If you experience little rain, check your worship life because, with the measure you use, it will be measured back to you. (Luke 6:38), little worship = little rain.

Intensity (quality) of rain – High-intensity rain produces larger size raindrops. The opposite is also true in that low-intensity rain produces small size drops. It is said that this high-intensity rain carries high energy and produces more impact. Rain and shower are not the same. Technically, a shower is a type of rain. It is usually on and off with gaps of dryness, which results in unstable weather. This type of weather makes it difficult to plan your day due to uncertainty. To experience continuous wet weather, you need a downpour of rain for hours at a time. A worshipper can experience spitting, drizzling, showers, sprinkles of rain or a larger size outpouring of rain. The high-intensity worship will result in a deluge, overwhelming rain of God, which will produce energy that propels a worshipper to make an impact for God.

Duration (sustainability) of rain – Rain can be short or long. In some parts of the word, the rain can continue for three days or more. In an environment that is not prepared for a long duration of rain, they usually suffer destruction because the system is not set-up to handle the amount of rain experienced. The desert does not give up moisture; hence, it does not experience rain. It is important to experience continuous rain so that the soil of our life is continuously replenished, we can bear fruit, and our fruit will abide.

Frequency of rain - The frequency of the rain or how often we experience rain depends on how much and how often moisture is evaporated from the earth. During my years of working as a contractor, as I drove around, occasionally, I drove into the rain and out of the rain. Some people's experiences are summed up in Amos 4:7, which reads, "I also withheld rain from you, when there were still three months to the harvest. I made it rain on one city; I withheld rain from another city. One part was rained upon, and where it did not rain, the part withered."

---- **66** ----

An occasional worshipper will have occasional rain, the intermittent worshipper will experience intermittent rain, but continuous worship brings continuous rain.

---- **99** ----

Why do we need the rain?

Rain – A source of freshwater

Rain is a source of freshwater for drinking, which has the potential to hydrate and brings refreshing to the body. Water is essential to life, and it is the divine source of all living things.

According to Greek philosopher Thale, water is the real substance of soul and nature. John 7:37-39, "Now on the last day, the great day of the feast, Jesus stood and cried out, saying, 'if anyone is thirsty, let him come to Me and drink'. He who believes in Me, as the scripture said, 'From His innermost being will flow rivers of living water. But this He spoke of the Spirit, whom those who believed in Him were to receive; for the Spirit was not yet given because Jesus was not yet glorified.'" 70% of our body is water, 83% of our blood is water, 75% of the brain is water and 79% of the heart is water. If major organs in the body are mainly water and for the body to be in full operation as designed, it needs 70% water. As a believer, you cannot do without God's rain because a body cannot perform at full capacity when it's running on 30%. Rain adds water to streams, lakes and rivers and keeps alive the animals in the sea. Worship keeps a believer's spirit alive to God; it keeps a believer fresh continually and influences all areas of their life.

Rain washes

The rain can wash anything dirty. One of the functions of water in the body is to help remove toxic waste that can harm our body. In all activities of daily living, we need water to wash not only ourselves but the laundry and dishes too. I remember that sometimes in the spring when the external part of my car is dirty, then it rains, the rain makes the car look cleaner than it was before the rain fell. Acts 3:19 says, "Repent, then and turn to God, so that your sins may be wiped out, that times of refreshing may come from the Lord." Burdens are lifted when we worship, and we feel renewed. Worship also allows us to be vulnerable before God in surrender, asking Him to cleanse us from all unrighteousness.

Rain is required for productivity

Rain is needed for productivity. For example, water is needed to make our daily meal, and in some parts of the word, they depend on rain due to underdeveloped infrastructure. The level of productivity of a believer is commensurate to their worship of God. This is not the same as attending a church service. In Deuteronomy, God said to the children of Israel that if they serve or worship other gods, He will shut up heaven and there will be no rain and no produce for their land (Deut11:17). Rain is needed for farming and for rearing livestock (they need green grass to graze). Farmers look forward to the rainy season because rain breaks up the fallow ground, softens the soil and allows the seed sowed to open up in the soil so growth can take place. Our worship life must be intact to be a productive believer.

Rain impacts on climate and temperature

The rain affects the warming of the air, can alter time and can impact the rise in sea levels. Rain gives a cooling effect in summer after high temperatures. Rain after days of snow can help to melt the snow. Also, the rain helps to reduce the intensity of cold weather. Water is stored as sweat on the body surface of the skin during warmer weather, and evaporation of this sweat gives the body a cooling effect. Worship regulates the weather of our life. Worship can dissolve fear, relieve stress, remove low mood and a confused state as we are reminded of the things He has done and what He promised He would do.

Rain is a power source

Flowing water creates energy that can be captured and turned into electricity. In a well-advanced society, hydroelectric power can be stored (pumped storage plant). Large amounts of water are needed to produce energy power; hence, most plants use a reservoir or a dam. I am especially excited about this because I know there is power generated as we worship. Our worship is a weapon of war to defeat the enemy, and as we continually create an atmosphere of worship, power is released to wage a good warfare. When the children of Israel were going to take Jericho, God said they should shout, and their shout brought down a formidable wall. In 2 Chronicles

20:21, King Jehoshaphat put the singer in front as they went to battle against Ammon, Moab and Mount Seir, and they worshipped God. The Lord set ambushes against these three nations, which came against the people of God and Ammon, Moab and Mount Seir, and they were defeated. Flowing water creates power, not stagnant water, even when water is stored in a reservoir. When it's time to generate power, the water is engineered using a turbine to create a flow that will create electricity.

Rain brings exchange

The rain causes the flow of minerals within the soil and the flow of minerals from land to sea and vice versa. In the body, the minerals obtained from food need to be dissolved in our body fluid (water) before it can be of benefit to the body. Worship causes an exchange to happen between heaven and earth. God comes, His presence comes, and He inhabits our worship. When a king comes to town, he comes with all his glory and goodness and gifts. The same thing happens when God comes to worship and fellowship with us – we are never the same.

The Rainbow

The sky lightens up after the rain, and sometimes a rainbow is seen in the sky. A rainbow is said to be a phenomenon no one can fully understand.

It is an arc of colour that can be seen in the sky. We are taught that there are seven colours of the rainbow. Scientists said that a rainbow is caused when light is reflected (mirroring) or dispersed (act or process of distributing a thing over a wide area) in water droplets. Worship exposes us to God's light, and as we stay around that light, we begin to mirror that light. The light of God is distributed to all areas of our life and dispels every darkness; we see better and further. The rainbow sometimes is seen after a storm, although it is after a storm, it is beautiful to behold and makes the sky colourful. When you worship during the storm, there is a rainbow to bring colour to your life because God never forgets His covenant and He cannot fail.

The giver of Rain

To experience the rain, you must know the giver of rain. This is beyond salvation. When you know God, you know His spirit because the Holy Spirit is the spirit of God. Hosea uses the analogy of rain to explain the result we get when we know God. Hosea 6:3 says, "Let us **know**, let us **press** on to know the Lord; His going forth is **prepared** as the morning; and **He shall come unto us as the rain**, as the latter and former rain unto the earth" (KJ200). This version says when I **know** God and I put pressure (**press**) on myself to know Him, God is **prepared** (past tense) to come unto me like the rain.

The international standard version says it even clearer, Hosea 6:3, "Let us **strive to know** the Lord. His **appearance is as sure** as the dawn. **He will come to us like the rain,** like the spring showers that water the land." To strive means to **fight vigorously** to achieve a thing. This suggests to me that a laid back, lukewarm attitude will not bring the rain – we must fight for it. Philippians 3:10 (Contemporary English Version) says, "All I want is to know Christ and to experience the power of His resurrection, to share in His sufferings and become like Him in His death."

When you know God, you will worship Him. The more you worship Him, the more of Him you know; it's a never-ending cycle. To know a thing means to be conscious of it, to be intimate with it and to latch on to something. As we fight vigorously to know God, our faces are not covered. They show the bright glory of the Lord as the Lord's spirit makes (transforms) us more and more like our glorious Lord (2 Corinthians 3:18 CMV).

When we fail to worship God, we experience spiritual drought and famine; a believer will dry up on the inside. Famine can manifest as lack, deficiency, insufficiency, poverty and shortage in different areas of our life. You want the rain; you want God to come to your aid; then fight vigorously to know Him. Don't blame God if stuff happened and He did not show up as you expected because God has no business coming to your aid if you don't know Him.

——————————— " ———————————

God is merciful, and sometimes He will give you a miracle to draw you to Himself, but He is not your jackpot or vending machine.
He created you to worship Him.

——————————— " ———————————

The extravagant God

My God is excessive
200,000 species of animals He created
He filled the sea with numerous species of
fish
Just because He is God

My God is extreme
He owns the storehouse of snow
He takes darkness to its home
And opens the door for light in the morning

My God is elaborate
He created the stars
He calls each star by name
And they appear in order

My God is classy, flashy and posh
He built a city for Himself
He made the wall jasper
The street pure Gold

My God shines with Glory
He sparkles like precious stone
He is clear as crystal
His glory illuminates me

His love for me is outrageous
He is unreserved in His blessing
He lavishes me with His goodness
His love is unexplainable

He paid the price already
For you to experience His priceless gift
His costly blood was shed
To bring you closer to Him

Lay down your pride and irrational thought,
Embrace this extravagant God
His blood is gushing with forgiveness, all
you have to do is say yes.

Get to know him

If you have offered God strange worship and you want to come back to Him, or you don't know Him at all, please pray this prayer and mean it in your heart:

Lord Jesus

I thank You that I was in Your mind

When You died on the cross

You shed Your blood for me

To make a way for me to worship You

I confess my sins today, and I ask You, Jesus

To forgive me and cleanse me from all unrighteousness

I receive You, Jesus, into my heart to be my Lord and Saviour

I promise to love You, to serve You and to follow You

For the rest of my life, in Jesus' name

Amen.

Welcome into the family of God! The past is gone, the new is here. If this is your first time of saying this prayer, please let somebody know you decided to follow Jesus. Find a Bible-believing church, and get yourself planted and rooted in Him as a true worshipper.

Printed in Great Britain
by Amazon

84812598R10039